I0115682

A QUICK AND PRACTICAL GUIDE
FOR BUYING
YOUR NEW HOME

Mary Ann Pollock, MS

A QUICK AND PRACTICAL GUIDE FOR BUYING YOUR NEW HOME
Copyright © 2015 by Mary Ann Pollock, MS

All rights reserved. No part of this publication may be reproduced, distributed, or transmitted in any form or by any means, including photocopying, recording, or other electronic or mechanical methods, without the prior written permission of the author. Exceptions are made for brief quotations embodied in critical reviews and certain other noncommercial uses permitted by copyright law.

Disclaimer: Although the author and publisher have made every effort to ensure that the information in this book was correct at press time, the author and publisher do not assume and hereby disclaim any liability to any party for any loss, damage, or disruption caused by errors or omissions, whether such errors or omissions result from negligence, accident, or any other cause. The information is not intended to be professional advice, but only as a guide to remind readers to exercise due diligence under the circumstances.

Reliance on or use of the information contained in this publication are at the reader's own risk. Homebuyers and other readers should consult the appropriate professionals for advice and assistance when making their decisions.

To contact the author, Mary Ann Pollock:
  Email..........: mapcat9@hotmail.com

Printed in the United States of America
ISBN 978-0-9908265-1-4 Paperback
-Self Help   -Personal Growth

Cover Design – Bobbie Fox Fratangelo
Author Photo – Susan Hope Finley

CONTENTS

CONTENTS

DEDICATION

This book is dedicated to my family, friends, and mentors who have helped me persevere to the completion of this book. My hope is that this information will serve home-owners now and in the future.

As a new homeowner, you can enjoy the privilege of fresh, safe, and unlimited drinking water. Most people throughout the world do not have access to safe water for their daily needs. A portion of the proceeds from this book will be donated to build water wells in the United States and abroad through Living Waters for the World.
(www.LivingWatersForTheWorld.org)

INTRODUCTION

Buying a home is an exciting, interesting, and challenging life event. The purpose of this book is to assist you in purchasing your first home and possibly others. Whether it is a condominium in the city, a house in the suburbs, or a cottage by the water, careful consideration will help you find the right place to live and avoid costly mistakes. My hope is that the facts, tips, and ideas contained herein will help guide you to the right place!

HOW TO USE THIS BOOK

This book is designed to make your life easier as you consider purchasing a new house. It will help you consider the full picture surrounding the purchase of any specific house. The book contains handy checklists as well as tips about credit, mortgage applications, and moving day.

Read through the book carefully, and then slip it into your pocket. Use the checklists as you view any home. Each question will guide you to answer in one of three ways:

- Yes
- No
- Deal Breaker (D.B.)

> *Here's kind of my motto—if you're not happy at home, you're not happy anywhere else.*
>
> ~ *Angie Harmon*

COMMUNITY AND GEOGRAPHY

Evaluate any house in the context of the community that surrounds it. The perfect *house* is not necessarily the perfect *home* for your family. The perfect home is a great house in a community that fits your family and meets your needs.

As you evaluate a house, consider the following questions:

	YES	NO	D.B.
Do the physical conditions invite a sense of community?			
Are people and pets outside?			
Will the demographics of this neighborhood match your family?			
If you have school age children, are other children likely to live in this neighborhood?			
Does the reputation of the school meet your requirements?			
Will bus stops be convenient?			
Is this location convenient for your commute to work, grocery shopping, day care, or religious community?			
Is this house subject to any condominium or homeowner association bylaws? If so, what story do these tell you about your potential neighbors, and what will be required of you as a resident?			

Are the crime statistics for this community acceptable to you?			
Does the community have a neighborhood crime watch?			

Everyone says I'm like the girl next-door . . . .
Y'all must have really weird neighbors!

~ Kelly Clarkson

BASEMENT

If the basement is flawed, don't fall in love with the house!

Inspect the basement first. While the basement is the least romantic part of any house, it contains the structure and guts of the house. If the basement has major problems you can't afford to fix, LEAVE without exploring the remainder of the house.

Do not allow yourself to buy a house you can't afford to bring up to standard. Falling in love with the kitchen or the family room can cloud your judgment and lead you to a purchase a home that becomes a maintenance nightmare. If the basement is flawed beyond your ability to fix it, don't even look at the rest of the house.

Take your flashlight and check the following items in the basement:

Foundation and Joists

	YES	NO	D.B.
Are ceilings uncomfortably low?			
Is there adequate head room as you traverse down the stairs?			
Do crawl spaces have access areas for service?			
Have crawl spaces been sealed to deter pests from entering?			
Have floor joists been insulated?			
Do floor joists or basement windows show evidence of pest infestation?			

Walls and Corners

	YES	NO	D.B.
Do you see evidence of dampness?			
Are gutters and downspouts diverting water away from the foundation?			
Are tree roots preventing drainage?			
Is there any evidence of water infiltration into the basement: peeling paint or wallpaper, rust, stained walls or floors, discoloration?			
Do floor coverings show evidence of mold or mildew?			
Has the house been waterproofed?			
If the house has been waterproofed, does the homeowner have a written guarantee?			
Do any of the basement walls have cracks? Are any bowing or buckling?			

Heating Unit

	YES	NO	D.B.
Does the house have a hot water or forced air heating system?			
How old is the unit?			
Has the unit been upgraded to a high-efficiency model?			
Do you see evidence of rust or other problems?			

Air Conditioning

	YES	NO	D.B.
How old is the unit?			
Has the unit been upgraded to a high-efficiency model?			
Do you see evidence of rust or other problems?			

Plumbing and Hot Water

	YES	NO	D.B.
What type of plumbing exists? Has old piping been updated?			
Is the capacity of the hot water heater large enough for your family? How old is the unit? Do you see evidence of rust?			
Does the hot water tank have a drip leg to release water?			
Are the drains located properly to avoid water damage?			
Is there a utility sink in which to wash paintbrushes and pets?			

Basement Windows

	YES	NO	D.B.
Are basement windows stable?			
Do they need to be caulked and insulated?			
Do windows provide security and privacy? (Glass block windows provide both.)			

Electrical

	YES	NO	D.B.
Does the electric service have capacity to meet your needs?			
Do the current owner's major electrical loads match your expected use? (For example, if the current owner has a gas dryer, and you have an electric one, you may need to buy a new gas dryer or have an electrician install a new circuit for your current electric dryer.)			
Do you see evidence of rust or other problems in the electrical panel?			
Is the cable coming from the electric meter into the electrical panel in good condition?			

Decorate your home. It gives the illusion that your life is more interesting than it really is.

~ Charles M. Schulz

OUTSIDE THE HOME

The outside of a home and the property on which it sits can be a thing of beauty that brings you great pleasure. It can also present a time-consuming maintenance task.

Be sure to look at a property from outside at different times of the day. Visit after a rain or storm.

As you look at the home from the outside, consider the following questions:

Roof

	YES	NO	D.B.
What is the age of the roof? Are the shingles in good shape? Are they secure, curling, or moss covered?			
If slate, is a supply of slate on site for repairs?			
Are soffit and fascia boards along the roofline in good repair?			
Do overhanging tree branches pose a risk for damage?			
Is flashing (usually metal pieces) in place around the chimney base?			
Are gutters and downspouts in good repair? Do they divert water away from the home's foundation to protect from water damage? Are they free of leaves and debris?			

Pest Control

	YES	NO	D.B.
Does a check of the outside wood show infestation of birds or insects?			
Does the house have an open porch or stoop framework that may invite birds, wasps, or hornet nests?			
Could missing siding or peeling paint be an entryway for pests?			

Garage, Driveway, and Sidewalks

	YES	NO	D.B.
Is the house equipped with a garage or carport? (Although a carport reduces wear and tear on the car and protects from weather, an integral or attached garage provides the most security and convenience.)			
Does the garage suit your current and future needs? Can you manage any steps involved? Are handrails securely in place?			
Would backing into the garage provide additional room to load and unload your vehicle?			
Are the electrical outlets in the garage sufficient and up to date?			

Is there an outside water faucet?			
Is the driveway on your property? Is it shared with a neighbor?			
Are you prepared for snow removal on this driveway?			
Are sidewalks safe and in good repair?			

Foundation and General Outside Appearance

	YES	NO	D.B.
Do you see any missing siding, gutters, downspouts, shutters, shingles, or peeling paint?			
Does the foundation look stable from the outside? Do you see evidence of tree root damage?			
What is the age and condition of the windows? Are screens in place? Do you see any broken windows in the home, basement, garage, or out build-ings?			
Does the mortar on a brick home show signs of age or loose joints?			

Other Outside Amenities

	YES	NO	D.B.
Can you locate the electric, gas, cable, phone, water, and sewer lines? Ask about current maintenance contracts on any of the lines. If so, can the seller provide information on the contracts?			
Are there outside water faucets and electrical outlets? If so, are they in working order?			
Is there a swimming pool? (Whether in the ground or above ground, swimming pools require maintenance and insurance. They also pose resale considerations.)			
Are there any sheds, gazebos, or other moveable structures? (These may or may not be included in the sale.)			
Is there a fence to keep your children or pets safe, or to keep you safe from neighbors' pets? If so, is the fence in good repair? Who owns and maintains the fence?			

An hour of sleep before midnight is worth two hours of sleep after.

~ Kenneth H. Pollock, author's father

Lawns, Trees, and Everything Green

There are three seasons of home ownership: raking, shoveling, and mowing. If you have an aversion to these, consider the cost of lawn care or buy a condo!

	YES	NO	D.B.
Are you prepared to care for the property? Are you willing to mow grass or pay for the service? Will your existing equipment do the job?			
Will trees or shrubs on the property line need to be trimmed? If so, determine who is responsible.			
How are shrubs, trees, or vines located in relation to the foundation? Is the foundation block secure to prevent damage inside the structure? Are the lawn plantings likely to carry insects into the home?			
Do blooming flowers and shrubs create a welcoming ambiance to the property? If so, are they located near entranceways where bees could become a concern? Do any of your family members have special needs regarding allergies to plants or insects?			

INSIDE THE HOME

Kitchen

The kitchen is the center of the home. Use your imagination to envision your family functioning in this kitchen. Imagine preparing food, eating meals, entertaining, and hosting holidays in this space.

	YES	NO	D.B.
Do you love the sight and feel of the kitchen? Can you imagine your family enjoying this space?			
Is the kitchen large enough to meet your present and future needs?			
Is the natural lighting in this room bright or gloomy? Is this kitchen a cheerful space?			
Do the doorways and configuration allow for a smooth flow? How will traffic flow when you're are serving food and entertaining?			
Are appliances included in the sale price? If so, open them for inspection. Check for age and good working order. Make a note to request warranties and operating manuals.			
When do you estimate the appliances will need to be replaced?			
Is the counter height comfortable?			

Is cupboard space sufficient?			
Are there sufficient electrical outlets for your current and future needs?			
What does a look under the sink tell you? Is the area under the sink free of water damage? Check for the age and wear of the plumbing.			
What does an investigation of the water tell you? Check for water pressure, smell, and taste. Find out if there is a water conditioning system in the house. If so, be sure to find out the monthly operating cost.			
Will it be difficult to keep floor coverings, counter tops, and appliances clean and well maintained?			
Will the table and furniture you own fit in this kitchen? If not, where will it go?			
Does a careful investigation reveal any hidden problems? Move rugs and items on the counter top to check for problems.			
What changes will you need to make for this to be a dream kitchen? Are those changes within your budget?			

A house is not a home unless it contains food and fire for the mind as well as the body.

~ Benjamin Franklin

Entryways

	YES	NO	D.B.
Is the guest entryway warm and inviting?			
Is the coat closet adequate?			
Is there a convenient powder room for guests?			
Is there a mudroom for family members?			
Are the doors strong and secure?			
Are entrances large enough to move furniture in and out? Could entrances be remodeled for handicap access?			

Bathrooms

	YES	NO	D.B.
Are there enough bathrooms for your family to live comfortably?			
Is access to plumbing readily available for repairs?			
Is the water pressure in sink and tub adequate?			
Does the toilet flush well?			
Are bathrooms free of evidence of water damage or deferred maintenance? For example, is the caulking around the bathtub, shower, and sink in place?			

What does an inspection inside the toilet tank lid reveal? What is the water quality inside the tank?			
Could a bathroom be adapted should a family member be injured? (Accidents or health issues can occur during any season of homeownership.)			
Do you need to make changes to feel comfortable with the bathrooms in this house? Are those changes within your budget?			

Living Room or Great Room

	YES	NO	D.B.
Does this room feel inviting and comfortable to you?			
Will the shape of this room accommodate your furniture and lifestyle?			
Is the natural lighting in this room bright or gloomy?			
Can you envision your Christmas tree or other holiday decorations here?			
Are there sufficient electrical and cable outlets for your current and future needs?			
Can you expand or adapt this room for future needs?			
What changes will you need to make to be happy with the living areas in this home? Are those changes within your budget?			

Bedrooms

	YES	NO	D.B.
Does the number and size of bedrooms meet your family's needs? (Remember that the main function of a bedroom is sleeping. In most cases, buying a house with a larger kitchen and living areas is more important and promotes resale better than large bedrooms.)			
Are there sufficient electrical and cable outlets for your current and future needs?			
Is there adequate closet space in each bedroom?			
Will your furniture work in these bedrooms?			
What changes will you need to make to be comfortable with the bedrooms in this house? Are those changes within your budget?			

Conserve water while brushing your teeth by turning off the faucet,
> *~ Esther M. Pollock, author's mother*

Second Floor Living Space

	YES	NO	D.B.
Can you locate emergency exits from the upstairs windows?			
Are the furnace and hot/cold vents sufficient for your needs? In colder weather, will there be adequate heat to this floor?			
If the house is without central air conditioning, can window air conditioners be readily installed?			
Are there sufficient electrical outlets for your current and future needs?			

Attic

	YES	NO	D.B.
Is there sufficient insulation for heating and cooling?			
Do you see evidence of water damage or pest infestation?			
Is there an attic fan to cool the house and save on air conditioning costs? If so, is the fan in good condition?			
Is there safe and convenient access to the attic?			
Does the attic provide adequate storage space?			

Crawl Space

	YES	NO	D.B.
Does the height and opening of the crawl space allow for convenient access?			
Is this area easily accessible for repair of the main operating elements of the home?			
Is the area secure from pests and water?			

Other Physical Considerations

	YES	NO	D.B.
How wide are the stairways? Are the treads easy to walk? Can you move furniture through these stairways?			
What are the ceiling heights in the home?			
What is the condition of the walls throughout the home? Are cracks or crumbing a sign of serious problems?			
What is the condition of the windows? What is their insulation value? Do you feel drafts around the windows? Do all the windows open and close with ease? How difficult will the windows be to clean?			

GUIDELINES FOR GOOD CREDIT

A good credit rating is important throughout your adult life. A good credit rating is an important asset that no one can take away from you. You never know what opportunities or obstacles could occur that may require an application for credit.

Use the following tips throughout your credit journey.

- Always live and borrow beneath your present means. This not only protects your credit rating, it makes it easier for you to sleep at night.

- Create a 5, 10, and 20-year life plan, and manage your finances and credit accordingly. Revise your plans with life changes.

- Make payments on time. Slow or delinquent credit can cause increases in home and auto insurance rates.

- Before you buy an item, pause and think about whether you need the item. Could a gently used article be substituted for a new item?

- Review your credit report annually to determine validity of data reported. Free credit reports are available from various agencies.

- Pay your credit cards in full monthly. Carry balances only for extremes or major purchases (medical, home, or car repairs). Unless you can pay off the account in full when the bill comes, do not use a credit card for clothing, entertainment, or food. If you will not be able to pay for an item in full when the credit card bill comes due, ask yourself if you really need the item now.

- Avoid applying for credit cards at multiple stores. Having many open accounts negatively impacts your overall credit score.

- Do everything possible to avoid filing for bankruptcy. If you do file, the credit implications will follow you for the next several years! Your credit life will be on hold until the waiting period ends. If you need credit during or after a bankruptcy, you may be charged higher interest rates.

Mortgage Credit Application Information

Many types of financing are available to you as a consumer. In every case, many documents are required to apply. Some of these include, but are not limited to, name and address of employer(s), pay stubs, two years of completed income tax returns, two months of bank statements, and all pages of the contract. You might also be required to submit divorce/separation/child support documents, evidence of the recent contract or sale of a present home, credit card/student loan payment statements, and/or documentation of employment changes.

At the time you apply for financing, provide the following to the loan officer:

- The name you prefer to use on all documents. As you are signing legal documents, your given name is the best name. (Be sure to sign your name in the same manner throughout the entire process.)

- Any credit history you have under another name.

- Copies of your social security card, driver's license, passport, or other photo identification.

- A complete paper trail for any funds you received as a gift for the purchase of a house. In most cases, cash is not acceptable. Documents must state that such funds are gifts rather than loans.

- Documentation for any relocation assistance given by your employer. Inquire through your human resource department.

- The zoning classification of the property.

Additional Tips:

- Prior to applying for a mortgage, be sure that all fees related to a real estate transaction are specific and clearly stated in the contract.

- Investigate the possibility of government down payment assistance in the area. Check with the local municipal officer or realtor for information where the house is located.

- If repairs are required on the property prior to closing, do not proceed to closing until the issues are resolved. An executed addendum to the purchase contract may be required.

- Be aware that the lender is not responsible for contractors chosen to work on your property prior to closing. Be sure to get references. If a contractor repairing or remodeling a home is not acceptable to you, it is your responsibility to insist on a change. If repairs are financed, speak with your lender about any problems.

- Once closing is complete, it is your responsibility to make your first payment on time. Sometimes the first payment is due before a payment book or statement is received. At closing, be sure to obtain a copy of the payment amount, name, and address of lender.

- Receiving approval for your loan does not necessarily mean that all parties are ready to close. Your loan closing may be delayed due to weather related issues, availability of the seller, repairs, vacations, and holidays.

REAL ESTATE PURCHASE TIDBITS

- Sleep on the decision to sign any contract. Once you sign, you become legally liable. This applies to all contracts, including property sales, credit cards, rent, leases, and other purchases.

- Read, read, and re-read your contract. Put the contract aside and read it again.

- Ask questions and then ask more questions. Don't stop asking questions until you are confident you have reached full understanding.

- Consider making your offer to purchase a house contingent on a home inspection by a licensed professional of your choice. Although you will have to pay for the inspection, it can save you money. Negotiate with the seller or realtor over any major issues.

- Be present during your home inspection and learn all you can about the condition of the house. Ask questions.

- Give a down payment at the minimum amount for the purchase price involved. Be prepared to verify the source of down payment funds.

- Know your realtor and the firm he or she represents. Real estate is a competitive business. Always protect your own interests.

- Have the title of any property you wish to purchase reviewed, either by your lender or the title attorney where the closing will take place. Make sure the property is free of liens and unencumbered by any of the following: divorce in process, held in trust, estates, or other pending legal action. Any of these issues could delay your closing.

- Purchasing a title insurance policy should prevent future problems with the title of your home. You can obtain this insurance through the title attorney performing the closing.

- Check for easements for shared driveways. If one is not on record, get one! Private roads may not be eligible for financing.

- Keep life insurance policies updated. Be sure your life insurance policy is appropriate for this change in your financial obligations. Update your will as well. Be sure an appropriate individual knows where these documents are kept.

- Investigate homeowners insurance to fit your needs. Disclose any fireplaces, wood stoves, alternative heat sources, or other unique features of the property to your insurance company. Review your home insurance needs with the agent approximately every five years.

- Take special precautions for estate sales. Check to see if the estate has been processed through probate court. Make sure the estate is in a position to sell the property. Make certain there are no existing liens.

- Take special precautions for distressed sales. Review title/legal work to determine if the sales price will cover existing liens. Ask yourself if you are prepared to wait out the repairs and/or legal issues. These may take a while to resolve. Be realistic.

- Consider land contract sales as another financing tool. Consult a legal advisor when choosing this option.

- Determine if a road right of way exists. Widening of a road could reduce frontage, change driveways, and change property value.

Moving Day Adventure

The big day is on the horizon! Consider the following tips for a smooth transition to your new home:

- Be sure that your homeowners insurance will be in place at closing.

- Be sure that all utilities will be transferred to your name by moving date.

- Obtain keys, garage door remotes, and security alarm codes.

- Before you leave your old home, create a video of furniture placement and belongings. Create another video or chart of where you want the items placed at the new location. (This information could also be provided to your insurance agent to update coverage.)

- Prepare for the needs of your pets relative to the move. Remember their health records in addition to food, bowls, leashes, and other paraphernalia.

- Organize items so that you'll have what you need to use them. For example, an electronic docking station requires the cords and remotes. Musical instruments are played with music.

- Prepare for immediate kitchen and bath needs. Pack paper and cloth towels, soap, and hand sanitizer so they will be readily accessible.

- Do not forget the toilet tissue!

- Plan food and beverages for moving day. Make sure disposable cups, napkins, plates, and trash bags will be readily accessible. Fruit, cold/hot drinks, snacks, sandwiches, or a slow cooker recipe will provide meals for a busy day.

- Use colored folders to track important documents, lists, and essential information that could be misplaced in the move.

- As you prepare for the move, save and recycle plastic storage bags for small items. These include cords, knick-knacks, desk supplies, and kitchen and bath products.

- Be sure you have a supply of blankets, throw rugs, tarps, or carpet remnants readily accessible. These help save floors and assist with covering and moving your possessions.

- Pack serving utensils and flatware. Use of disposable or recyclable items will save you time later.

- Be prepared to set up the bedrooms first at the new home. Wash or freshen linens in advance. Prepared bedrooms will be a relief for everyone at the end of a long moving day.

WITS, WISDOM, AND COURTESY

- Trust in God, but lock your doors.

- Keep flashlights, batteries, portable radios, candles, and fire extinguishers available and in good working order.

- Install smoke detectors on all floors. Check your batteries in January and June.

- Use either a safe deposit box or fireproof safe for important documents. Be sure a trusted person knows the location of box and keys.

- Take severe weather advisories seriously. If you have a basement, go to it. If not, move to a safe place away from windows. Don't wait until it's too late.

- Consider winter weather when installing outside holiday decorations. It may take until a spring thaw to remove them.

- Keep an inventory of your belongings so they can be replaced if stolen or destroyed by fire or flood.

- Keep emergency telephone numbers in a central location.

- Report vandalized mail boxes to authorities to prevent reoccurrences and possible break-ins.

- Seek out community information for special health needs from Welcome Wagon or social service agencies.

- Place a house key in a safe place or with a trusted friend in case you misplace the key in your pocket.

- Display house numbers on your mailbox and home. Repairmen, friends, and ambulance drivers can find you more easily.

- Fly your flag. Have the kids help raise it. This is a good tradition to establish.

- Keep petty cash at home for garage sales and Girl Scout cookie sales.

- Shovel your neighbors' sidewalks when you shovel your own.

- Check on neighbors during or after bad weather.

- Admire your neighbor's holiday decorations when you wish them Happy New Year.

- Mind your own business, unless the neighbor's business is a threat to yours.

- Check for pet laws in your new community. Promptly obtain required licenses.

- Plant roses on the south side of a house.

- Be gentle with the earth you own and around you.

- Start a compost pile.

- Open windows facing south and north to create a natural breeze in summer months.

- Be cautious about planting flowers near a door way. They might invite insects inside.

- Buy a good leaf rake, garden rake, and spading shovel. Cleaning after each use will make them last a long time. These tools are great for retrieving balls or disposing of pests.

- Buy a good garden hose and nozzle.

- Own more than one bucket.

- Hang a bird feeder where it can easily be seen. A good spot is near the kitchen.

- Reduce the insect population by inviting bats and purple martin with appropriate houses.

- Recycle used Christmas trees.

- Sweep your garage regularly. This will help the house will stay cleaner.

- Use rugs at entryways and shake them away from the entrances.

- Close the garage door to keep leaves from blowing inside.

- Follow the local rules for recycling. Use the proper receptacles.

- Be responsible for your trashcans. If the wind blows a can into the street, it is your responsibility.

- Get to know the local gas station owner. If this person cannot repair your vehicle, he or she will know who can.

- Meet the local pharmacist. You may need him or her for advice and/or emergencies.

Buy, buy, says the sign in the shop window; why, why says the junk in the yard.

~ Paul McCartney

ABOUT THE AUTHOR

With over 25 years of mortgage lending experience, Mary Ann Pollock has a considerable amount of knowledge and insight regarding home buying. She is an FHA licensed underwriter, with extensive experience in the processing and closing of real estate loans. Mary Ann is also a licensed notary public for the State of Ohio.

Mary Ann holds a Master of Science in Organizational Leadership and a Bachelor of Science in Business Management. She is a member of the Columbiana Board of Zoning Appeal and Columbiana Business and Professional Women.

Mary Ann supports Living Waters for the World (www.LivingWatersForTheWorld.org).

Her interests include learning new things, experiencing new adventures, and serving others through various church and community activities.

www.ingramcontent.com/pod-product-compliance
Lightning Source LLC
Chambersburg PA
CBHW060701280326
41933CB00012B/2262

9780990826514